FOOTBALL ARTS INITIATIVE

KOP STORIES

Heartfelt and humorous terrace verse

by

Dave Kirby & Nicky Allt

Illustrations by Mike Burrows

A House of Scouse publication
by Allt & Kirby

All proceeds from this book will go to the
Hillsborough Justice Campaign
and Zoe's Place baby hospice

Printed by Flexipress Ormskirk

Foreword by Mike Myers

'Alright there Wayne's World - you nugget' - these were the first words I heard Dave Kirby and Nicky Allt utter as I sat comfortably on the inter city train about to depart Lime Street Station for London Euston. My immediate thoughts had me contemplating the usual Austin Powers follow-up, but I was surprised when the two of them sat at the adjoining table before Nicky spoke. 'So Myers me oul flower; are you really a Kopite, or were you just blagging your way around Scouseland? Before I could proffer an answer, his question was rapidly followed by the Kirby fellers probing, 'a Canadian Kopite eh - now you don't get many of those to the Yankee dollar.' Once I could get a word in edgeways, I was immeasurably pleased to find that the guys were both LFC nuts like me. And so passed a fantastic three hour train journey as they regaled me with their tales of football travels gone by, while I went about reassuring them that my dads' main objective for leaving Liverpool was not simply to fulfil a lifetime ambition of joining the Mounties.

I'd been literally exhausted on boarding the train, but their infectious humour and tales of red triumph soon lifted me from the doldrums, wherein, I almost wished the journey would never end.

On arriving in 'The Cockney Gaff' as they called it, I had a chauffer driven limousine waiting to take me to Heathrow Airport; it would have picked me up in Liverpool where I'd been visiting family, but I declined the offer of a boring motorway ride as I wanted to witness the forty shades of green from a train window - my own favourite mode of transport. As Austin himself would have said, 'A spiffing choo-choo jaunt through England's green and pleasant land.' After an on-board beverage or three we departed the Station to meet Harry the limo driver, who after much hearty laughter, parked his said vehicle outside the supping tavern known locally as The Gardeners Arms. Once ensconced, and half inebriated I may add, inside this Cockney boozer (the lads' description) the time literally flew by and so did my blooming plane. Harry, noticing I was worse for wear, took me on to the Dorchester Hotel for the night, and basically from there on in I can't remember anything about the cab ride, the hotel lobby, disrobing, not to mention the wibbly wobbly water bed or the flowery, Laura Ashley type wallpapered room I awoke in the next morning - hmm - Scouse reunion parties eh.

A few weeks later and I received a call to my agents' office from the two Road End rascals (their description, not mine) asking if I'd be kind enough to write a foreword for a coming venture in verse they had planned; well boyos...here it is. Hollywood superstar or not, I demand my free copy and an invite to the next derby game, providing I'm not earning megabucks - you know how it is...I hope. So, without furthermore ado, relax and enjoy the words of my two drinking hosts, my two fellow red nuggets and my two Scouse buddies. Oh, and by the way boys, Harry sends his best and was wondering if you'd seen his hat and a pair of binoculars usually locked away in the backseat compartment. From myself and in the words of Wayne's World, 'Rock-tastic my little beauties' Toodaloo you guys and come on you groovy rhyming reds.

ps...where's my free copy?

pps...Binoculars and hat please

Mike Myers (The Canadian Kopite)

Kirkby La La

Nicky Allt

These semi-surreal sets of verse were written purposely in a non-highbrow, simplistic rhyming tone; the kind of verse that's as basic as basic can be (bit like the football special buffet tray) - get me - or in other words, in the Scouse vernacular of an eighteen year old young tear-arse. I don't profess to be an academic man of verse and never will; that's too far up ones arse if yer knowarramean. For myself and Dave, writing and a lot of the arts are usually in the hands or the domain of the middle classes, and one of our main objectives in taking up the pen was to try and write things for ordinary, everyday people. Too many times you find yourself reading about things you know about or have lived through, only to find the facts distorted or totally misleading due to the author not having much of a Mr. Magoo about what he's writing about, or football wise - not knowing the difference between Larry Lloyds undies and Phil Thompsons hankie. It's for this same reason that most theatres are half empty and most TV programmes bore me witless with a capital SH. If I ever find an audience to take the writing further, then it's to my own brethren I take aim.

Soon my first big book (The Boys from the Mersey) will be on the shelves and if it is decently received then I hope to go on from there. A play co-written with Dave called 'Brick up the Mersey Tunnels' is also in the pipeline, but whether or not anybody has the foresight to go with the production is another matter. Both of us were raised in an environment not usually accepting to artistic venture, so I think we both put the writing on hold for twenty years till we eventually arrived at this spot in time. Anyway, enough rattle about me and thee, and from two Kirkby kids now storied-up, travelled-up and ready to blow, here's a few little ditties to keep under your bed with your oul Adidas Samba. Oh, and by the way, when I hitchhiked to my first away-game and the older lads were laughing at me because I was trying to rob ollies at Keele service station, without a shadow, nobody could have foreseen that I would one day become a real life Yozzer Hughes with a pen - 'Go on, gizz some ink, I can write that, go on soft shite, gizza biro, I can scribble that.' See yer iffa get there. Nicky...

Oh yeah - An' don't go all serious on me - they were only written for fun.

Dave Kirby with young Tom McFadden whose father's memory inspired the poem "The Homemade Flag"

Until a few years ago I hadn't written anything sincere since I was twelve. That was mainly down to being 'ripped' for having poems published when I was at school so I developed another style... 'taking the piss'. Understandably, it was the only kind of verse that lads from my environment could handle, and continued throughout my many years in the building trade.

The change came when I saw a Hillsboro related poem called 'that lad' by Peter Etherington. It moved me to write a piece called 'The Homemade Flag' about a childhood mate who tragically died aged 36. It proved a big turning point. (nice one, Tommy, lad). After a couple of years attending workshops at JMU and writing/performing for radio, I moved on to writing drama and have recently completed a novel. Most of my Kop stories featured here have appeared in fanzines and websites over the past few years, but I've left the Chubby Brown type ones for another time. The humorous pieces come from Nicky.

For Nicky and me writing is a compulsion. Many aspects of our characters help drive us on, but one we definitely share is our upbringing in Kirkby. Its semi rural location mixed with inner city culture made it a diverse and creative town to grow up in. Let's face it - there aren't many fellas who can say they've lashed bird's eggs at away fans at the match. Anyway, enough blag, let's begin where it all started..... on the terraces of the old boys pen.

Dave Kirby

THE OLD 'BOYS PEN'

It's fifteen minutes to kick off time
I'm in my seat, Block 109
I look around, I hear the noise
see lots of fathers with their boys.

The kids look happy a marvellous sight
Macdonald's burgers they all bite
they're all excited that's for sure
and with their dads they feel secure.

Although the surroundings have now all changed
the children's feelings are still the same
the middle classes have now arrived
but things were different for a sixties child.

I then look out across the kop
to the right hand corner at the top
where up until the age of ten
I served my time in the old 'boys pen'.

For those of you who do not know
it was a place for kids to go
metal bars like a kind of cage
where little kopites came of age.

I remember the first time I went inside
Liverpool v Chelsea 65
a star struck boy who stood amazed
football was all we had those days.

You'd always see some kids from school
they came from all over Liverpool
little scousers every week
from Kirkby town right up to Speke.

The kop was packed out in those days
but at half time, dad found a way
to fight his way through all the crowd
and feed his boy, he did me proud.

An 'Eccles cake' a sausage roll
a drink of coke, god bless his soul
between the bars he'd pass it through
like feeding monkeys at the zoo.

And through those bars we used to stare
at all the kopites standing there
oh how we'd long to stand with them
and make that step from boys to men.

Some kids escaped now and again
it was a pretty dangerous game
it filled the kopites full of laughter
to see kids dangling from the rafters.

It had its own 'soprano' choir
you couldn't sing 'walk on' much higher
inside those bars kids sang with pride
but it sounded so funny from the other side.

When the match was over at 4.45
your dad would pick you up outside
dozens of kids some big some small
stood opposite the pen by the old brick wall.

But that was how it was those days
no greedy players no corporate ways
they recognized us 'kopite cubs'
we were the future of the club.

Then at last it came my time
to leave this little world behind
I was at an age where every lad
didn't want to go the match with dad.

And so I passed out to the kop
that love affair has never stopped
I take my son to the occasional game
but this 'dad and lad' thing's not the same.

You never see young lads no more
who go the match in threes and fours
this city's children rue the day
when they took the old boys pen away.

The money men arrived in town
and in their wisdom pulled it down
they called it 'progress' but we read their thoughts
who needs children when adults pay more.

I now drift back to present day
I take my seat, watch the red men play
a diehard red, I'm the real McCoy
because I was groomed from a little boy.

That golden era has now passed by
but we all have memories you cannot buy
from apprentice kopites, now middle aged men
who served their time in the old boys pen.

Dave Kirby

Mike Burrows

Lizzie, Lizzie please tell me -
How come its never Sir Bob. (Smiths title)
(If yer all love the royals clap yer hands.........silence)

The only true king of the North East
The greatest manager - ever been born
While Queenie reads out the honours-list
We sit and laugh - full of scorn

Let's start with Sir Elton John an' his rent-boys
A battered arsehole an' sacks of cocaine
While Sir Bob fought in tanks for his country
The Rocket-Mans playing the Dame

Candle in the wind fer Diana
Now the Yellow Brick Roads upped an' gone
It's all fer charity thee tells us
But ferrim - its still number one

Once again...he's bang in the limelight
I loved her he yelps - he's a sir
But we can see through those gold glasses
An' under that new head of hair

Then there's Rolling Stone - Sir Michael Jagger
He's had more Brown Sugar than most
Been caught gooseing more times than Rodney
While buttering Skag on his toast.

The Lips an' Keith Richards have dabbled
But at least Keith admits his part in the scene
While Mick prances round with his balls hanging out
While sidling up ter the Queen

Meanwhile Bob's as clean as a whistle
A Gentleman (slow) sturdy an' proud
A World War veteran an' rooms full'er trophies
D'yer whannus ter shout irr'out loud?

13

Take Sir Bobby Robson fer instance
A nice fella - as far as it goes
But I've seen more cups won at Tranmere
Yerree's wearing the Gentleman's clothes

Sir Bobby this and Sir Bobby that
Bit of a joke - yill agree
There's only one Sir Bobby in our house
And that's Sir BOB PAISLEY

Take a look at Sir Alex McTaggart
He's called Sir for being a Manc
Now - sure - I know he's won trophies
But let's have it straight...he's a crank

Spitting on the floor and talking shite
While the blotchiness spreads round his gob
Telling lies for Shergar Nistlerooy
Who we all know is one cheating knob.

Now let's not be biased on this point
Even the Beatles have had a good bash
With McCartney locked up in a Japanese Nick
Sir Paul...should read...Sir Stash

But at least the man's got the talent
And keeps any vices well hidden
While Jagger and Fergy ride with the devil
And Elton...well he just gets ridden.

Bobby Charlton got his for fringe-benefits
And for pushing his barnet across
Cos Preston became a shit football team
When they made Bobby they're boss

Nah - there's only one real Sir Bobby
Bob Paisley - a soldier - a man
Ten years the boss at Liverpool
Just ten years ter win all yer can

No waiting around - year after year
No daft, five-year blags, fer him
No second chances in the Champions league
Where even when you're beaten - yer win

It's a birrova lottery this Sir game
Waiting fer the sound of a gong
Where phoneys can come before Gentlemen
By pickin them up ferra song

In ten-years it'll be the money-mad Keegan
With Gareth an' Will storming up on the wings
One - a shit manager from Yorkshire
In a race with the Karaoke kings.

The race ter be a Sir's already started
With a load of oul blaggers in tow
When Queenie reads out the new honours list
Ter gerronit - which way d'yer go.

D'yer get yerself right in the limelight
Ter tell everyone yer such a great man
While shagging all the brasses that fame brings
Or snorting all the Charlie yer can.

Maybe we'll get Sir Gary Lineker?
Or maybe Sir Jonathan woss?
I can just imagine thee headline
HONOURS LIST - Woss is the boss.

D'yer start licking the boots of the aristocracy?
Or live as decadently as yer possibly can?
Keep chopping up pigs in the abattoir
Cos soon you'll be Sir Boiled Ham

Yer know am messin...but in me eyes it's a joke this Sir game
A lottery...where phoneys can win
While people like Sir Bob lived an honest life
While the phoney Sir's live it - in sin

I'll say it again fer the deafened
He spent his fittest days at the war
But lived ter become Libpools manager
And went on ter win prizes galore

The greatest manager in all the land
Sir Bob Paisley - remember his name
A man who lived honourably an' gloriously
Without ever playing fer fame

Now that's a true-Sir by quite a mile
Any nous and I'm sure yill agree
So let's shout all the way ter the Palace
For a man called Sir Bob Paisley.

So (slowly) Queenie and all of her entourage
Have created a true British farce
So where phoneys and losers win prizes
Yer can stick yer Honours List - RIGHT UP YER ARSE

THE END - Royalty an'na know yeah - HA!
In fact - double fucken HA!

Nicky Allt

Mike Burrows.

POOR SCOUSER TOMMY
(THE UNTOLD STORY)

Near Bootle docks in a terraced street
where kids played football in bare feet
stands little Tommy, 8 years of age
most kids were poor in pre war days.

They'd have to borrow, beg or steal
and rarely ate a decent meal
but no one held their heads in shame
for kids back then were all the same.

Together with his little mates
he'd peer through the dockyard gates
at merchant ships from far and wide
who's cargo's had them hypnotized.

As Tommy grew into his teens
he'd make a shilling by any means
he'd steal from Peter to pay back Paul
to watch his hometown play football.

To Anfield every other week
he'd amble through the cobbled streets
climbing gas lamps with dirty hands
stealing apples and skipping trams.

Like all young lads he had no cares
life is such bliss when your unaware
one big adventure from day to day
just eat and sleep and steal and play.

For boys like Tommy knew not their fate
a world wide conflict lay in wait
their youth was halted in its tracks
as war torn Europe faced Hitler's wrath.

The sound of cheering and waving rattles
would soon be swapped for guns and battles
aged just 19, who would have guessed
he'd soon do battle with Rommel's best

Together with his older brother
he kissed the cheek of his tear-filled mother
in his uniform with his packet of fags
and his lucky red hat in his old kit bag.

Then off he went on a southbound train
en-route to the battle of El Alamein
to the royal artillery he was commissioned
with the 51st Gordon Highland Division.

He arrived in October of 42
as Monty's 8th army were turning the screw
but nothing prepared him for what was to come
in the blistering searing north African sun

They were given their orders to relieve the front-line
but the path to Tripoli was laden with mines
so they'd all split up into 12 man platoons
then tip toe with death through the minefields and dunes.

There was just no escaping the sweltering sun
or the deafening noise of the bresa guns
there were flies in their thousands and nothing but sand
in this god forsaken war torn land.

They came to a clearing by a salt marsh trail
where a battle enraged on a frightening scale
the shell fire was deafening as smoke filled the sky
Tommy muttered a prayer "Lord don't let me die."

He reached in his pocket for his lucky red hat
things were looking real bad for these desert rats
the German panzers had attacked from both flanks
leaving smouldering corpses of burnt out tanks.

Then orders were given by Tommy's command
to gain high ground and make a stand
he kissed his hat as he put it away
then advanced with his troop on his final day.

In the mayhem which followed on that hot afternoon
there was all but 2 of his 12 man platoon
they were trapped in a crater left by a shell
all around lay the bodies of those who had fell.

The soldier with Tommy was hit and in pain
his trembling hand held his cross and chain
he said 'Get me home' with a tear in his eye
'Just leave it to scouse' came Tommy's reply.

So amidst the screeching of mortars and shells
he decided to dash through this living hell
he took a deep breath, closed his eyes
touched his hat once again then climbed over the rise.

But Tommy's dash would be ill fated
as death's dark angel calmly waited
for as he stood to make his run
he was sprayed with bullets from an old nazi gun.

He danced in a death like a marionette
falling back in the crater from which he'd just left
his injured friend crawled across where he lay
but the bright burning sun was now fading to grey.

As the blood from his head wound flowed into the sand
his weakening grip dropped the hat from his hand
the lucky red hat which he treasured so much
lay tattered and bloodstained in the African dust.

Then visions flashed before his eyes
of his Liverpool home, and times gone by
his tearful mother, and his childhood mates
waved up to the sky from the dockyard gates.

It was at this point just before he died
that he turned to the soldier by his side
he reached out a hand, pulled him near
then whispered his last words into his ear.

The month was January of 43
about 20 miles east of Tripoli
in the blistering heat there was something cold
it was the body of a boy just 20 years old.

The last words he uttered through his dying breath
are a lasting legacy to Tommy's death
some 60 years after his heavenly call
his words are now folk law sang by us all.

The sacrifices that those boys made
seem long forgotten by folk these days
they died so we could all be free
they died for the likes of you and me.

So every time we sing that song
we'll try and remember right from wrongs
we'll sing it loud and recall with pride
poor scouser Tommy, and the millions who died.

Dave Kirby

SPECIALS ON SPECIALS -
Never a train in vain. (Clash title)
(Winter, cold morning an' thee FA Cup)

On a hundred Satdee mornins
When I could'er stayed warm in me flock
I'd be down with the lads on platform nine
Under the Lime Street clock.

That big oul train would rumble on in
With everyone up on their toes
The doors clanging open the startin bell
With just enough room ter land blows

The battle was on ferra flea-ridden seat
And ter park the arse of yer jeans
While most lads were dreaming of a five-nil win
Some harboured naughtier dreams

A few young lads boarded that Special
Fighting for seats that were sparse
With the F.A. Cup, only half of the dream
And the other of Mary's big-arse

Let me explain.
Yersee, legend has-it, it was just lads who made the trip
On the way ter see the Red-men play
But a few Mary-Ellens were aboard that train
And thee didn't push the buffet-tray.

CHORUS
It was all Mars Bars, crisps an' shitty meat pies
As basic, as basic can be
But meeting Mary-Ellen in Limey that day
Made the whole trip worth it fer me.

We were playing Southend in the F. A. Cup.
A night-match - due ter the snow.
I boarded the Special with an arm in plaster.
An' returned with more than a glow.

Comin home me toes were frozen in me Samba
With me heart pounding under me Fred
Tell yer...by the time we got back to Limey
Her scanties weren't the only thing red

Yersee, it was my time to meet Mary-Ellen
Who the older lads had told me about
With a snorkel hanging up on the toilet door
Where thee'd felt-tipped a warning - KEEP-OUT.

The Bizzies usually stuck me in the cage
But here I was stuck in the bogs
200 miles through thee English snow
Standing there - free frim me togs.

With a broken-arm set in plaster
In a shithouse where yer couldn't swing a cat
When Mary showed me her Mary
I didn't give a fuck about that.

CHORUS
All Mars Bars, crisps an' shitty meat pies
As basic as basic can be
But meeting Mary-Ellen on the Special that day
Made the whole-trip worth it fer me.

We'd beaten the Southend easily
We were in the big-hat fer the draw
The next round couldn't come quick enough
Like me...behind that closed-door

I'd eard about joinin the mile-high club
But that was a game fer the rich
Now it was all - Lois pulled down - and arses ter the windder
And her not wearing a stitch

We'd started are own little sex-game
Called 'Specials on Specials' by us
While wandering who we'd get in the 4th round
I straightened me togs without fuss.

'I'll see yer in the next round Mary'
'If yer lucky, soft-shite' she said,
Yersee being the James Bond of the Special
Had instantly gone ter me head.

Well...here I was thinking I'm John Holmes
The porno-scally of the track
While I was just a rip in her knicker elastic
Another young prick from the pack.

CHORUS
All Mars Bars, crisps an' shitty meat pies
As basic as basic can be
But meeting Mary-Ellen on the train that day
Made the whole-trip worth it fer me.

I only add one more special with Mary
At Spurs when Terry Mac scored that lob
It was the goal of the season by a mile' n a half
D'yer remember that look on his gob?

Well I add that look leavin Euston
As me kecks once again hit the deck
While the fans were singing and dancing
I left the bogs like a wreck

(Slow) It was the second lob knocking about that day
As I walked down the train with a smile
Little did I know it was the last lob
That I'd see on that train ferra while

I searched for Mary-Ellen fer years after that
Me football Special looked over fer good
Till the mid-eighties an' older an' wiser
Ordinary to West Ham - I'm hit wirra thud

Sitting there comfy an' cosy
It's Mary - football-kitten supreme
As I winked at her, she winked right back
'Walk the buffet, while I find the cream'

CHORUS
Mars Bars, crisps an' shitty meat pies
As basic as basic can be
But meeting Mary-Ellen in the carriage that day
Made the whole-trip worth it for me

Reaching the buffet I waited fer her,
'Hello girl - how's things - member me?'
She said, 'yeah - but wharra yer after?'
I said, 'Gerrin' eer an' we'll see.'

Pointing to the bogs - she clocked the door
'You've gorra cheek don't yer think'
'But I was thinking we'd pretend it's the Special,
An' you'd get yer arse in the sink'

When she smiled, I thought I was laughin
And that Specials on Specials was back
She looked in me eyes, 'in yer dreams big-boy'
'You'll find me fellas back down the track.'

Not wishing ter be arrivv order
I said...'How's about a ham-shank'
'All good things must pass soft-lad'
'Now keep what yivv gorrin the bank.'

'Oh, yer mean fer Ipswich away next-week?'
'No soft-shite (pause) fer never again'
'But Mary, it's a long way ter London
An' a think I'm already Big Ben

CHORUS
All Mars Bars, crisps an' shitty meat pies
As basic as basic can be
But seeing Mary-Ellen on the ordinary that day
Made the whole-trip worth it for me

No more Specials on Specials forever
I suppose we all af'ter grow-up
Though whenever I think of Mary-Ellen
In a jiffy I'm 'up fer the cup.'

A hundred league titles and Europe
I went to most on that flea-ridden train
But once Mary-Ellen got married
The journey was never the same

A bit of how's yer father on the way ter the match
Made the Specials special fer me
With Liverpool reaching every goal in sight
While I reached fer the big double D

Maybe it's the oul rose tinted glasses
Cos jumpin off at Edge Hill's all we could afford
But Mary turned the special inter the Orient express
When she pulled me emergency cord

Now it's all luxury cars an' van-hire
An' traffic-jams cause nottin but pain
I'd swap all that comfortable travel
Ferra seat on that flea-ridden train

It was like going on a football adventure
With a cattle-truck of scallies in town
A hard-case, a dresser, a loud-arse,
A fanatic, a nut-case, a clown

Every character was aboard that choo-choo
Satdee morning - platform nine - bang on cue
But please don't forget Mary-Ellen
Cos Kop kitten was always there too

CHORUS
All Mars Bars, crisps an' shitty meat pies
As basic - as basic can be
I'd let Black-beard lock me in that cage right now
(Pause) If Mary-Ellen was waiting for me.

The End - Red Marksy's scanties - St. Micheals
specials - Where are yer girl?

Nicky Allt

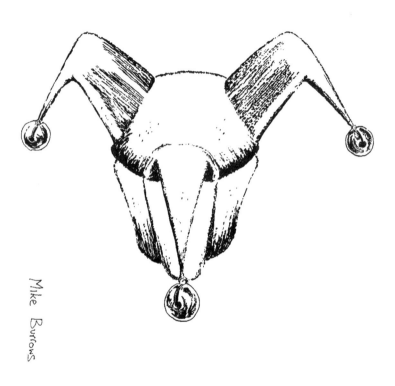

Mike Burrows

JESTERS HATS

I'm sitting underneath the kop
with my little six year old lad
I look in his eyes, and I see that gleam
the one that I once had.

And then he pulls me by the sleeve
and points at a fella in red
then he sits and stares at the Jesters hat
that he's wearing on his head.

So I just shake my head and frown
at the way that football's gone
I mean...I know the reasons why it's changed
and I know that times move on.

It's just that every now and then
when I'm with my lad at the match
I wish for one day I could take him back
to the days before Jesters hats.

To the ones when everyone got the bus
and paid in at the gate
when the kids sat on your shoulders
or stood on a wooden crate.

There weren't any fast food burger bars
Or close circuit TV
and no one tried to rip you off
with £2 cups of tea.

And the banter from the kop back then
sort of captivates a time
when the city was filled with characters
and the humour and the wit were sublime.

You never heard songs like 'You what, you what, you what'
I'm talking about songs with soul
sang by Dockers and labourers, and sparks
and brickies... or lads off the dole.

There was something about that atmosphere
that you don't get anymore
it was working class and passionate
and genuine and raw.

And it was mainly always scousers
who used to fill the ground
there wasn't any middle class
or people from out of town.

But now they come from everywhere
and I haven't got a problem with that
it's just that it hurts when I think of the days
the days before Jesters hats.

So my lad finishes off his big Mac meal
and he grabs his little flag
then we head upstairs and take our seats
inside the 'Dad and lad.'

Then I look round at the other kids
all sitting with their Da's
and see lads my age whose childhood seat
was an old kop terrace bar.

Our nineteen seventies hairstyles
are now receded or laced with grey
it seems like us old Kop terrace boys
have long since had our day.

Sometimes it's hard to accept the fact
that you're slowly getting old
especially when you measure your life
round the fields of Anfield road.

You think of Wembley, Paris, and Rome
and they seem like yesterday
but then you realise that twenty-odd years
have somehow slipped away.

So then the final whistle blows
and I grab my little lad's hand
I wanna tell him the way the Kop once was
but he wouldn't understand.

And I know that the seats are safe and sound
and I wouldn't want it any other way
it'd just be nice to take him back
if only for just one day.

So then we filter out the ground
with all the other reds
and I know he'll dream about the match
tonight when he's in bed.

And as he sleeps I'll hold his hand
and have a quiet chat
then I'll give him a hug, and a little kiss
as he dreams about jesters hats.

Dave Kirby

Mike Burrows

ELEVEN RED TOILET ATTENDANTS

If you ever waltzed through the Anfield turnies
In the mid-nineties more or less
You'd have found eleven shithouse attendants
All trying ter mop up the mess

Yersee, we've all gorrar our worst footballers
Who the Reds've signed on the dot.
But thinkin about Souness an' Evans
It was the red-route ter losing the plot.

From Dead legs Stewart to nutty Piechnik
An' Calamity James our space invader king
That divvy punched fresh-air every corner
Instead've one-trick Walters out on the wing

D'yer remember 'Is he in the Van Kozma'
He and that Jimmy Carter were alike
They had abbar three games between them
Before the abrupt 'gerron yer bike'

Then came the guitarist from Abba
'Benny Kvarme' his Norwegian name
He defended like a Viking Dancing Queen
For Evo it was 'The Name Of the Game'

Up stepped WHOOSH! From Bristol
When Nicky Tanner brought his boots
The lad'd be dreaming when the other team scored
Cos he'd forgotten to dye his roots

We soon bought a Cockney wide boy
Razor Ruddock cigar in hand
He'd light one up on the halfway line
When he appeared in 'no mans land'

Souey tried ter sign The Terminator
When he and Boersma went the flicks
But he'd signed a deal in Hollywood
So we got Julian Dicks

We had Dundee biscuits an' model Matteo
And James Bond Scales who could give it a lump
With the gorgeous rinse of Jason McAteer
And the mangy left foot of Stig of the dump.

Up popped Deano from the Beano
Like Billy the Whizz he could run all day
A bit like Leo Leonhardsen
But thee couldn't play the Liverpool way

I'm sorry to inflict some pain here
By having ter mention those white suits
When Phil Babb walked out at Wembley
Wearing his... Air-Wair boots

He'd slip; he'd slide and then eat the soil
With no Hansen class, or style
Then slap his balls against the post
Ter try and raise a smile

We did our best ter sell him to anyone
But we could hardly raise fifteen pence
Tranmere offered two pound ninety-nine
Till in stepped a Portuguese fence

The Sporting Lisbon man paid up in citrus fruit
The deal was heaven sent
Cos we all knew how shite he was
An' that he couldn't trap a bag of cement

He was swimming around the Algarve
And we didn't give two hoots
Cos he'd never look right, upon the beach
In a cozzy and Air Wair boots

Soon the Sunderland boys came inter the frame
When Peter Reid stepped in
But relegation soon showed its face
When he made him, their lynchpin.

He stepped out fer the Mackems
New boots and a lovely tan
The lad should've stayed where he belonged
Inside an ice-cream van

Our very own Eddie the Eagle
Who passed like he was standing on ski's
We haven't had many bad footballers
But he was the worst by a mile fer me

slower
Yep......I'd say he's the worst by a Kop roof'n a half
Phil Babb, Air Wair boots, bar none
No more bogus ball-players wearing the Red
Now all the Shithouse Attendants have gone.

Please lord, WE ARE Liverpool - no more fraudulent
footballers eh...Nicky Allt

Mike Burrows

THE HOMEMADE FLAG

In all the years we've been apart
I thought that time would heal my heart
but the hurt came back just yesterday
it never really goes away.

Came back from Cardiff full of joy
I hugged my daughter and little boy
I ask this question again and again
why weren't you spared to do the same.

My mind drifts back into the past
some thirty years it's gone so fast
two teenage boys whole lives ahead
off down to Wembley draped in red.

A homemade flag we took that day
it's incomparable to today
an old bed sheet, a bottle of dye
about eight foot long and four foot high.

It took so long to make that thing
scissors, cotton you would bring
every evening after school
sewing on the letters of Liverpool.

Down to London, midnight train
attempts to sleep were all in vain
Euston is cold at four a.m.
that flag came in handy once again.

Snuggled in our flag like peas in a pod
at 6-45 we were woken by plod
'Wake up now boys, you can't sleep there'
so off on the tube to Trafalgar square.

Only 8 a.m. but oh what a sight
Trafalgar was bouncing as if it were night
the black and white Geordies the Liverpool red
as the statue of Nelson looked on overhead.

About 300 strong we then marched without malice
through admiralty arch to Buckingham palace
'Let's wake up the Queen' you said for a joke
with our flag tied around you like batman's cloak.

All day around London it was much the same theme
so proud of our city and the flag of our team
we hung it from buses, we hung it from trains
then as we hit Wembley up it went once again.

The whole day was perfect and so was our team
the most one sided final that I've ever seen
I can never forget the joy on your face
as we lifted the cup then we turned and embraced.

As the years went by and we grew into men
we'd meet up every now and then
we'd talk of old times and things we had done
the Exorcist, Jaws, and Band on the run.

I remember so vividly the day I found out
that God had called your number out
I thought of your parents, I thought of your John
I thought of your wife and your 3 year old son.

But death has no mercy, doesn't play by the rules
to take a man in his thirties is so very cruel
you fought it so hard, but always in vain
then the trumpets sounded and the angels came.

Some three years later I was round at my mums
looking through all the old photo albums
when my ma shouted up from the bottom of the stairs
'There's a bin bag of yours on the spare room chair.'

Inside the bag there were all sorts of things
old programmes, scarves, and a book called 'Kop kings'
ticket stubs, news clips, things I'd not seen for years
then I stumbled on something which reduced me to
tears.

I stared for a moment in disbelief
my whole body went weak overcome with grief
for there near the bottom of this old memory bag
folded up nice and neat was our homemade flag.

I closed my eyes as I opened it up
my heart was racing as I finally looked
I wept like a child as I kneeled on the floor
as I thought of that day back in 74.

I held it so tight as I whispered your name
Ah, Tommy I wish I could see you again
had I known it was here I'd have done my best
to drape it around you when they laid you to rest.

But alas, now it's mine and it always will be
when I open it out it's your face I can see
adventures and memories which will always last
that flag is my window into the past.

So, goodnight god bless, Tom until my next prayer
I know that your spirit is around somewhere
you could be millions of miles on some heavenly star
but when I'm holding our flag, you are never that far.

Tommy McFadden 1958-1995
Dave Kirby

Yer got yer education from The Kop.

Quick - climb arr'er the Boys pen
The three o'clock roar starts ter swell
You'll never Walk Alone has just lifted the roof
While we give the Bizzies pure-hell

The fence soon becomes the monkey bars
As' a struggle and fight ferra space
Twenty ter thirty young rag-arses
Are havin' a Spion Kop race.

Here comes Tommy Smith leadin the boys
Half of Anfields emblazoned in sun
The other half's shaded by the Spion Kop roof
The whistle - our starting-gun

As the stewards try ter'see kick-off
The break-out starts ter'begin
All the young urchins are up on the fence
Doing their bess'ter break-in

Gerrar the pen wirrits fences
Gerrin ter the Kop with the sway
Big Johns makin his comeback
Tosh always scores on the day

Officer Dibble's bizzie clocking us
While we're all bizzie clocking Tosh
Just ter see if he's up ferrit
Ter put the blue-shite under the cosh

47

CHORUS
Stevie Heighway's always runnin
John Toshack is always scorin
Can you hear the Kopites Roarin?
Toshack is our king.

May the best team win an' all that crap
Cos there's only one team on the field
With the roar'er the Kop and the red shirts
Its how victory is usually sealed

Come on Redmen - show this shite
Send them over the park with fuck-all
Emlyn's got the boys storming forward
We've just gorra beat Alan Ball

The ginger-haired bastard is brilliant
But so's Heighway who's bang on the ball
He's fouled but the ref doesn't blow
They score - now its backs ter the wall

The little copper tops buzzing
He's runnin the game on his own
And Tosh isn't getting no service
It's easy fer lanky-Labone.

They score again and we're two down
We're knackered we'll never get back
I'm praying the Kop won't stop singin
And we'll soon get the shite on the rack

The second-half we're kickin inter the Kop
We sing an' we dance an' we sway
Twenty minutes in - it's a Red onslaught
We attack - but we've still had no say

CHORUS
Stevie Heighway's always runnin
John Toshack is always scorin
Can you hear the Kopites Roarin?
Toshack is our king

Stevie takes the ball ter the by-line
With the Everton defenders in tow
He feints ter cross fer big Toshack
But twats the ball straight in the goal

The crowd goes nuts, I'm on shoulders
We scream together - one voice
Bally's looking jaded and clapped-out
While Stevie's a fuckin Rolls Royce

Bayin and singin and urgin
There's fifteen minutes ter go
We're chantin an' pleadin an equaliser
While they want the whistle ter go

Our Irish Rolls Royce goes off down the wing
Beatin man after man in the mud
He crosses the ball for big John
Who powers it home with a thud

The dirt is marked on his forhead
We sing and dance and we bay
The noise reaches crescendo
As the Reds show the blues how ter play

Surely no time fer the winner
But the leveller gives us the hope
I'll pray to anyone for a third red goal
A vicar - a Buddhist - a Pope

CHORUS
Stevie Heighway's always runnin
John Toshack is always scorin
Can you hear the Kopites Roarin?
Toshack is our King

'You'll Never Walk Alone' hits the roof
As thousands of scarves hit the air
2-2 now feels like a victory
While the half's gone by in a blare

Red-shirts just keep stormin forward
As the Kop scream and dance till the end
The blue-shite are stuck in their own half
Trying their bess'ter defend

Cally sends over a beauty
As the 'Walk On' sways ter the front
Surely we can't get the winner
Oh for a new Roger Hunt

Their goalie punches the ball out
While we suck the ball through the net
Till the fat lady sings with the whistle
This derby games norrover yet

We sing and we scream fer the winner
While the blues ang'on by a thread
A cross flies in from the Rolls Royce
Looking for Toshack in red

The goalie punches irrout again
A fine 2-2 draw and they'll boast
They're thinking it's all done an' dusted
But they didn't count on our red ghost

Christy Lawler the right back supreme
The ghost who no one can mark
Has volleyed the ball as sweet as can be
As we play the blues of the park.

CHORUS
Stevie Heighways always runnin
John Toshack is always scorin
Can you hear the Kopites roarin?
Toshack is our king

The whole of Anfield is bedlam
The Kopites ablaze with the red
25,000 are bouncing
It's the dream from which legend is fed

The ref blows the whistle its over
The greatest derby I've seen
We came for Toshack and Keegan
And got Lawler the poacher supreme

If yer name me a derby that's better
A bobble-hat, I'll swallow in one
And don't mention the double at Wembley
When the Reds beat the toffees 3-1

I'm talking about our sacred soil
The shrine, where dreams can come true
The Kop and the player's tergether
When we beat the blue shite 3-2

The End. Oh my god I'm flying off the stanchion,
Christy's got the winner.

Nicky Allt

Mike Burrows

OLD JIMMY

A hazy winter sunshine
braves the February cold
and lights up all the empty seats
inside the Kemlyn Road.

The shadows fade and then reveal
a figure on his own
there is no football here today
as old Jimmy sits alone.

A forceful smile cannot conceal
his lonely pensive mood
as decades pass before his eyes
in silent solitude.

He needs to be alone today
he needs the time and space
to say farewell forever
to this special sacred place.

He gazes out across the pitch
towards the Anfield Road
and sees the place where he first stood
when he was ten years old.

He thinks of how the times have changed
and how it's gone so fast
as visions flash before his eyes
with players from the past.

He sees a young Bob Paisley
running out onto the pitch
he saw him make his debut
back in 1946.

The fifties team then take the field
but he stares down at the floor
remembering the relegation year
of 1954.

But thoughts of Shanks and Liddell
soon make his gloom subside
the flying Scotsman's decade
saw the great man Bill, arrive.

The sun then shines upon the pitch
like gold on emerald green
Jimmy sits back, fixes his cap
then ventures back into his dreams.

He looks across at the tunnel
Ron Yeats is there at the front
followed by Smith, Ian St John
and his Idol, Sir Roger Hunt.

The atmosphere now is electric
the sixties are filled with emotion
the Kop sings along to Beatles songs
and the football is poetry in motion.

The seventies thoughts are amazing
Anfield was blessed with king Kevin
then goose bumps rise upon his arm
as he thinks of 77.

The night when the whole ground erupted
to the volcanic red and white sound
of "We shall not, we shall not be moved"
which lifted the roof off the ground.

Of all the matches Jimmy's seen
since he was a boy aged 10
he'll never forget the ecstasy
that night against St Etienne.

He smiles then thinks of the 80's
when trophies and legends were many
Rushie runs through, plays a one two
with the magic mercurial Kenny.

His thoughts turn to Beardsley and Aldo
and the brilliance which that team did bring
he then hears the tune from "Black beauty"
as Barnes does his stuff down the wing.

The nineties bring mixed emotions
as memories freeze with the cold
not such great times inside his mind
but maybe he's just getting old.

He closes his eyes for a moment
feels the back of his throat run dry
his old hands begin to tremble
for now he must say his goodbye.

His lips are pressed tight together
he covers his eyes with his hands
he's then overcome with emotion
as he sits all alone in the stand.

A lifetime of magical memories
has sadly now come to an end
he takes a deep breath then whispers
farewell to this life long friend.

He slowly turns up his coat collar
as he rises up to his feet
then thinks of his son and his grandson
who'll inherit his treasured old seat.

And now for the moment he's dreaded
as he leaves the place that he loves
a tear rolls through his white whiskers
which he dries on the back of his glove.

The shadows then fall on the Kemlyn
old Jimmy's time is now through
he stands for a while in an exit
turns around then fades out of view.

That night in the sky above Anfield
a new star shines down from above
it will stay for all eternity
to light up the place that it loves.

The warmth of its glow is forever
as it shines down on old Jimmy's lad
who stares at the sky from the kemlyn
when he thinks of his dear old dad.

Dave Kirby

Mike Burrows

THE PRESTON BIRDWATCHER

He shot, he scored
And all the pigeons roared
Brian Hall! Brian Hall!

He shot, he missed
The directors' arse he kissed
Brian Hall! Brian Hall!

This plastic Jock from Preston
Who played out on the wing
Went to uni ter study arse-licking
And ter hear the birdies sing

Little Bamber was his nickname
And he was soon doing his thing
The fullbacks would fall upon their arse
As he'd fly down the wing

The Kop would show they loved him
By rising up to sing
But he'd put a finger to his lips
So he could hear the birdies sing

Yersee he had no time for football chants
Or the joy that that could bring
He'd rather be camouflaged down in the woods
Where he could hear his birdies sing

He'd noticed down at Anfield Road
That no Robins would ever nest
And he'd have more chance of finding one
In the beard of Georgie Best

He climbed ter the top of the Spion Kop roof
Tersee the famous Liver Bird
But he dive-bombed like a Kestrel
When he got covered in pigeon turd

This place where he played his football
Had no trees fer chiming birds
It was full up with Dockers and Sailor's
Who'd never mince their words

DOCKER
Bird watching? Bird watching?
Play footy and ferget that shit
Get yerself down ter the Grafton
That's where yill get real Tit.

Little Bamber
But lads, think of the feathered ones
And all the joy they bring
Just take yourselves out t'country
And you'll hear the birdies sing

DOCKER
We're norrin thee English countryside
It's the Mersey Estuary, haven't yer heard
This is the place of rag-arse seagulls
An' getting covered in pigeon turd

This is called a picket line
Now put yer money in the box
Where collecting fer the striking families
Who've been laid off down the docks

Little Bamber

We don't want politics here at Anfield
You see it's not a football thing
We'd like to silence all you lefties
So I can hear the birdies sing

DOCKER

The Birdwatcher had climbed the ladder
Over twenty years or more
A full-degree in suckholing
Had riddled him to the core

Little Bamber

But lads this is a premiership stadium
Where profits are the king
Now go and collect somewhere else
So I can hear my birdies sing

DOCKER

This budgie's lost the plot
Were all politicians here
Were only collecting for the Dockers
So what's he got ter fear?

He's the same with the H.J.C.
He'd like ter block them too
Now if we all spoke like Parrots
He'd soon change his point of view

Little Bamber

I'm no Ostrich, I'm Brian Hall
My heads not buried in t'sand
Now let's discuss this down my local
It's called the Bird in Th'and

I'll tell you about my Clucking Ducks
And the Eagle who's the king
I'm sure you'll forget about politics
When you hear the birdies sing

DOCKER

I told yer he's in Cuckoo land
And tharrees never gonna listen terrus
So polish me oul steel toe-caps
I'm off ter Anfield on the bus

Yersee we've tried the tactful route
So he'll hear our Rally cry
Now it's time ter play Sylvester
On the hunt fer Tweety Pie

Some people don't wanna listen
No matter what yer say
The only speech they truly hear
Is the language of street affray

(Docker quietly)
If you were talking about garden privets
Add let birdseed Brian act the thrush
Burra don't mean tweeting merrily on high
I mean scragged in a thorny bush

slower
Yersee, I'd like to play at fullback
When little Bambers on the wing
An' I'd tackle him around about waist height
Then he'll hear his birdies sing.

Apolitical people - in a political city - get me.
NICKY ALLT
A bar in Slovenia

64

THE BADGE

There are many tales, from many trails
by reds who've travelled far
of wine and dance from Rome to France
where they've graced most every bar.

As tales unfold from young and old
you hear the strangest things
but none more so than the tales which flow
from a Dortmund bar one spring.

The beer flowed as we hit the road
on the eve before the game
our shouts and cheers rolled back the years
all together once again.

Some fat, some small, some thin, some tall
we're all now middle aged
but have burnt the oil on foreign soil
since the Billy Shankly days.

Twas an awesome sight on that brisky night
in the Dortmund market square
With the Alaves boys we danced to the noise
of the Samba everywhere.

We'd sing and dance, and then advance
through glazoned weary eyes
our dwindling crew was now but a few
we were dropping down like flies.

I remember then it was after ten
in a side street off the square
where a shimmering light first caught my sight
and seemed to lure me there.

The alley was dark as a hound dog barked
and howled at a pale blue moon
then a breeze unfurled, and gently swirled
all the litter which was strewn.

I stopped and paused as I heard the roar
of laughter song and dance
as something said inside my head
that I wasn't here by chance.

As I ventured down I heard the sound
of a piano's rag time tune
which rang out loud midst the smokey clouds
from the doors of this saloon

I rubbed my eyes as I stepped inside
I was seeing things for sure
all the men wore hats and silk cravats
like they did before the war.

Then through the crowd sat tall and proud
in the corner of the room
was a familiar bloke in hat and cloak
who was very smartly groomed.

He pulled a chair then called me there
so I walked as though hypnotized
then down I sat and began to chat
with this mysterious old guy.

'Hello there lad, how's your dad
haven't seen him for so long
and I aint seen you, since you were 2
back in 1961.'

His grace and charm, made me feel calm
as the beer and whisky flowed
I was mesmerized and warmed inside
by the stories which he told.

I was worse for drink so didn't think
too much about what he'd said
and the piano played and the bar room swayed
as we talked about the reds.

And then by chance I happened to glance
at a badge upon his chest
it was worn and old trimmed in gold
with an old style Liverpool crest.

He then revealed, this tiny shield
and placed it in my hand
'That's yours he said, from a grand old red
pretty soon you'll understand.'

I was so impressed by this little crest
looking down as I pinned it on
a voice wished me luck, but as I looked up
this mysterious man was gone.

Well I searched the place for his friendly face
but the old man was nowhere in sight
So I drank up my ale, picked up my tail
and decided to call it a night.

Next day I awoke full of whisky and smoke
then remembered the night before
thought it was a dream, till a little badge gleamed
from my shirt on the back of the door.

So I hopped in the shower and chilled for an hour
then set off to the square in the rain
all the kopites were soaked as they partied and joked
and sang with the boys from Spain.

They thought I was mad when I took all the lads
down the entry to show them the place
it was all boarded out and said 'Danger keep out
Derelict'... like the look on my face.

With strong German liquor my memory soon flickered
and forgot all this mystery
then later that night we went wild with delight
as the redmen made history.

We cashed in our marks and danced in the dark
while the stars did a Jig in the sky
all the bars in the Town watched the beer flow down
as the Liverpool boys drank them dry.

So the very next day the 17th of may
I finally arrived back home
took the badge from my chest to put with the rest
from Paris and Wembley and Rome.

I then heard a thump which made me jump
so I quickly dashed upstairs
by the wardrobe door all over the floor
there were photo's everywhere.

I tidied them up then happened to look
at a tattered old black and white
as I stood and stared, I began to hear
the piano from the pub that night.

I sat on the bed and shook my head
breaking out in a stone cold sweat
as I realised the man who'd shaken my hand
was the grandfather I'd never met.

My whole body shook as I took one more look
to the sound of an echoing laugh
for the badge on my chest was the same little crest
which he wore on this old photograph.

There are many tales from many trails
by reds who've travelled far
of wine and dance from Rome to France
where they've graced most every bar.

As tales unfold from young and old
you hear the strangest things
but none more so than the ghostly glow
from a Dortmund bar one spring.

Dave Kirby

The Ghost Of Billy Liddell

My picture of Billy Liddell
He's ten foot dressed in red
Stooping low among the flying boots
Where angels fear to tread

His short back' n side's haircut
Is all slicked back on top
A working class hero in every way
Revered by a baying Kop

After his bullet like headed winner
He'd leave the arena and make no fuss
Wash and change out of his muddy boots
To pay his fare on a local bus

Oh where are you ten-foot idol
No sports cars or golden braids
No mansions up in Southport
Where histories memory fades

Yersee, One day Billy took that bus ride
Only never ter return
And he got replaced by popstar's
Whose boot's I'd like ter burn

With kids called Brooklyn and Sapphire
And over fifty grand a week
Five Mercedes and a penthouse
With a grand towards the beak

These flash cunts don't play football
Thee bleed it till it's dry
They're mercenaries in all three kits
That thee know the kids'll buy

player
When I score a goal on telly
Read the message on my vest
It'll tell you about my website
And where you should invest

I've got gold bars for shin pads
With Prada calfskin boots
A Cartier diamond earring
Topped off with dyed blonde roots

My Versace cashmere tracksuit
Over a black Armani vest
Please don't push for autographs
See my agent, for that request

Narrator - faster
He weaves his way through the adoring kids
Ordinary people and he's their Don
Got to reach the city bright lights
To drink the champers till he's gone

The bouncers always know his face
Please to meet you - Hi - I'm John,
He loves this club called Backslappers
It's full of hangers-on

Speeding home he crashes the Porsche
And wakes up in the passenger seat
It's the ghost of Billy Liddell driving him
With steel toe-caps on his feet

Player - slower
You can't drive me in those
Is the first thing he has to say
And with the money that they paid you
Why d'you bother to even play?

ghost

Well I played cos I loved the red jersey
Then the people and the crack
But you fellers have stolen the game from them
So I've come to take it back

You've got to change your greedy ways
Said the ghost of football past
Heed my words - before it's too late
Cos this greed game just won't last

Your milking the game for all its worth
And even more when it goes out live
While Rupert your greedy agent
Parks another Merc out on the drive.

narrator

Two years later and still ignorant
To the words that Billy had said
A Stringfellow's chandelier
Came Crashing down upon his head

All the decadence and greed
As football sold its soul
A Thousand selfish popstars
Had finally took their toll

The fans who'd built the clubs up
With their loyalty lying in tatters
Stood helpless as the agents said
'Its only money that matters'

His hedonistic lifestyle
Had swizzled his bloated head
While he took no heed to warnings
Or the words that Billy had said

Eventually the whole lot caved-in
With the Football league as host
While rich designer football man
Would gallivant and boast

player
I'll find myself a new football club
With welcoming bright lights in that town
I'll hit the net come Saturday
And its there I'll wear my crown

That chandelier only cost ten grand
How dare it touch my head
I've paid more for the silken sheets
For the servants to make my bed

So my adoring little football fans
It's to you I raise this toast
About a silly dream I had one night
About Billy...Liddell's...ghost

Money-mad mercenaries an'all that.
Nicky Allt - bevvied in Europe again.

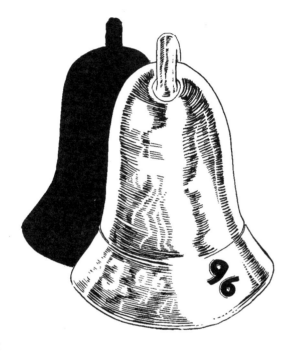

Mike Burrows

THE JUSTICE BELL

A schoolboy holds a leather ball
in a photograph on a bedroom wall
the bed is made, the curtains drawn
as silence greets the break of dawn.

The dusk gives way to morning light
revealing shades of red and white
which hang from posters locked in time
of the Liverpool team of 89.

Upon a pale white quilted sheet
a football kit is folded neat
with a yellow scarf, trimmed with red
and some football boots beside the bed.

In hope, the room awakes each day
to see the boy who used to play
but once again it wakes alone
for this young boy's not coming home.

Outside, the springtime fills the air
the smell of life is everywhere
viola's bloom and tulips grow
while daffodils dance heel to toe.

These should have been such special times
for a boy who'd now be in his prime
but spring forever turned to grey
in the Yorkshire sun that April day.

The clock was locked on 3.06
as sun shone down upon the pitch
lighting faces etched in pain
as death descended on Leppings Lane.

Between the bars an arm is raised
amidst a human tidal wave
a body too frail to fight for breath
is drowned below a sea of death.

His outstretched arm then disappears
to signal fifteen years of tears
as 96 souls of those who fell
await the toll of the justice bell.

Ever since that awful day
a vision often comes my way
I reach and grab his outstretched arm
then pull him up away from harm

I hear his voice, I see his face
but wishful dreams are soon replaced
by the vision which haunts me most
an empty seat on a silent coach

On April 15th every year
when all is calm and skies are clear
beneath a glowing Yorkshire moon
a lone Scots piper plays a tune.

The tune rings out the justice cause
then blows due west across the moors
it passes by the eternal flame
then engulfs a young boys picture frame.

His room is as it was that day
for fifteen years it's stayed that way
untouched and frozen forever in time
since that tragic day in 89.

And as it plays its haunting sound
tears are heard from miles around
they're tears from families of those who fell
awaiting the toll of the justice bell.

Dave Kirby

SOUTH YORKSHIRE POLICE

MikeBurrows

IMPUNITY FOR THE GUILTY

Each year in April when the daffodils grow
Inside my mind there's a place I go
It's a lonely place that's filled with tears
I've been going there now for 15 years.

I only visit once each spring
But I know the pain, which that place brings
I'm lucky I suppose, I can walk away
But the victim's families go there each day.

They've never been allowed to grieve
Justice faded with the funeral wreaths
A law once proud in a country once great
Lies broken and shattered at a cemetery gate.

There's a rotten stench that fills the air
Which smothers hope and brings despair
It clings to the skin of those who lied
And soils the memory of those who died.

The smell blows south to the Hampshire coast
To a hideaway where it clings to most
But the stench can never be concealed
While it clings to a man named Duckinfield.

It's difficult to understand
The arrogance inside this man
The selfishness that lies within
The lives he's ruined to save his skin.

No conscience, remorse, no guilt, no shame
Just gutless lies to shift the blame
Conveniently retired on grounds of health
To a peaceful life of untold wealth.

But what of those whose lives he failed
Why wasn't he tried, why wasn't he jailed?
Is the Hillsboro disaster a law apart
from the Selby rail crash, and Gary Hart.

Gross negligence and indecision
Were enough to send that man to prison
Involuntary manslaughter was his crime
Just like Duckinfield in 89.

But how can justice ever be
When the guilty are given impunity
The victims it seems will never find peace
While the guilty belong to South Yorkshire police.

Like John F Kennedy in 63
There are webs of lies and conspiracy
The tune of injustice is still being played
while Duckinfield dances on 96 graves.

His cowardly silence takes away hope
and spits in the face of innocent folk
he's not concerned with the torment it brings
not while the devil pulls on his strings.

Hey Duckinfield I want to know
On your pillow at night where do you go?
Do you see the visions, do you hear the screams
Do spirits visit you in your dreams.

Or are you glad you saved your neck
Do you think of your big fat pension cheque
Will you seek atonement, will you ever grieve
Will you finally bring closure to the families
bereaved?

Because for them the struggle each day goes on
A desperate fight to right the wrongs
their nightmare begins when they awake
just waiting in vane for the silence to break.

But until that time, each day they must go
To that lonely place where the daffodils grow
Where ninety six souls of young and old
Wait patiently in fields of gold.

Fifteen years since that tragic date
Fifteen years since he opened that gate
Fifteen years since he hid that tape
Fifteen years, and still they wait.

Dave Kirby.

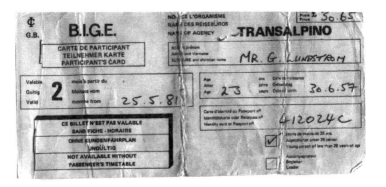

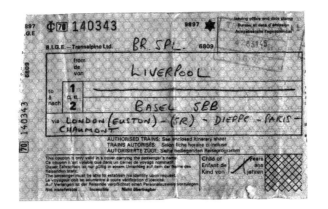

The Trans-Alpino Rub-Out Boy
(docket designer bar-none)

Yer know all those hoffmans down in Europe
Well I was determined not ter miss out
But I'd never have seen those European Cups
Wirrout the forged rub-out

I'd buy a ticket down to Oostende
Cos that's all yidd have ter get
Change the Oostende inter Munich
Tersee Ray Kennedy hit the net.

This one young master forger
Who'd do Dusseldorf ter Rome
Became Trans-Alpino rub-out boy
And its ferrim I write this poem.

He showed me the best techniques
An' in which pencils to invest
Up popped Borussia Moenchen
So I thought I'd purrit ter the test

A little birra rubbing up
Wirra little birra shade
By the time we reached the White Cliffs
We'd called it the Alan Whicker fade

(faster)
All 2 day trips, all 3 day trips
All 5 day trips, all six
We travelled where the fuck we wanted
With our little bag of tricks.

It's the stuff of Road End legend
I know...cos I was there
An' I paid me way ter Oostende
Ter breath in Roman air.

After Paris, Zurich, Munchen
Where we'd raised our banners high
New pre-season meant no rub-out
No matter how hard I'd try

Yersee the bastards had changed the tickets
The European boys were whacked
Some Road End lads just jibbed it
When rub-out boy got sacked

We got some mileage from that one
Those iffy tickets changed our lives
The cheapest travel by the length of Thommo's nose
Fer the under twenty-fives

Oh rub-out boy where are you?
I'm sure yer can sort the plane
Cos since we've used the airports
It's nowhere near the same

(faster)
No 3 day trips, no 4 day trips
No 5 day trips, no six
Now we're sitting on the plane with bizzies
An' a load of yokel pricks

The simple way of gettin there
With a toothbrush and twenty quid
Has been replaced by a membo an' an I.D. card
An' straight home ter watch the vid.

They're tryin ter lash us arrov Anfield
By the power of the pound
It's why the best support in all the land
Has lost its glorious sound

Present your visa cards fer tickets
From Cornwall ter Whitley Bay
But phone from Bootle or Kirkby
An' they're all sold out terday

No Road End scallies or Kopite skins
Who'd scream an' stamp an' shout
We've been shoved aside by the moneymen
Who'd like to rub - us - out

When I made it across the channel
With the arse hangin arrer me kecks
Me pockets were lined with pencils
And thee weren't fer signing cheques

No 3 day trips, no 4 day trips
No 5 day trips, no six
Its time ter get those pencils out
An' me scallywag bag of tricks

See - we're surrounded by arrer towners
Who were never on those boats
An add like them ter go back ter where they're from
In their brand new sheepskin coats

Once they'd infiltrated us
Ter try' an taste success
Soon they were imitating our speech
An how we used ter dress

But they're all just glory hunters
As far as I can see
An' I wished they'd leave my Liverpool
Alone fer you 'n me

If we could herd them onter trains
An' get them all aboard
We could lash thim off at Edge Hill
After I'd pulled the fucken cord

I know that sounds quite harsh
But a Scouser will understand
How we became quiet like all the rest
From being the noisiest in the land

No 2 day trips, no 3 day trips
No 4 day trips, no five
Oh rub-out boy please show your face
To bring our sound alive

One day we'll go ter Europe
An' the plane just won't go up
We won't be there on that glorious day
Ter see that European Cup

The pilot'll say we're all grounded
An' the lads'll be goin nuts
He'll say it's the weight of the platform soles
An' too many feather cuts

I don't like things watered down
Like our team and our support
Those arrer town glory hunters
Have weakened our big red fort

Our fortress once impregnable
Now almost has no sound
While the suits in the directors' box
Hear but the power of the pound

Slow down boy
No 3 day trips, no 4 day trips
No 5 day trips, no six,
Is there no chance of returning to cauldron days?
Among Anfield's hollow bricks.

slower
We know we've been hijacked by the woollies
Of that we're in no doubt
So rub-out boy come back to us
An'...rub...the...bastards...out

Another game - another woollyback moaner. Gimme
the crystal sound of scouse any day'er the week.
Niccolovitch Allt. TATTYBYE.

THE HILLSBOROUGH BANNER

The Hillsborough memorial banner was created in the immediate aftermath of the disaster on April 15th 1989. Its creators were Peter Carney, Fred Brown, John Fay & Tracy Ryan who used material that originated from a dis-used window dressing in Lewis's department store (Thanks Dicky). The names of each victim are listed on 17 league championship and four european cups painted either side of a Liver Bird. A blank european cup represents the victims of the Heysel stadium tragedy.

The banner was first exhibited on the wall of the Anfield Road/ Kemlyn Road exit of the ground as part of the great tribute, which covered Anfield in the weeks following the tragedy. Two more parts were added later using the same material. Part 3 (The baby banner) was created by Thelma Watson who stitched the full names of each victim around a circular floral pattern, which represents the aforementioned tribute. This part of the banner is on permanent display in the Hillsborough Justice campaign headquarters on Walton Breck Road.

As well as appearing at every home game during the season 1989/90, the banner was also displayed in the town hall, the Anglican Cathedral, Liverpool University and a number of music venues, and can be seen annually at the home game, which precedes the date of the disaster.

Particular thanks go to the M.P.A.C., The City Council and Trish for workshop help and continuous help. and a very special thanks to Alf Langley for his inspiration, then and now.

If you wish to know of any planned changes or would like to contribute to the refurbishment of the banners, please contact: Football Arts Initiative c/o 22 Helsby Road, Aintree, Liverpool. L9 4SH

John Alfred Anderson (62)
Colin Mark Ashcroft (19)
James Gary Aspinall (18)
Kester Roger Marcus Ball (16)
Gerard Bernard Patrick Baron (67)
Simon Bell (17)
Barry Sidney Bennett (26)
David John Benson (22)
David William Birtle (22)
Tony Bland (22)
Paul David Brady (21)
Andrew Mark Brookes (26)
Carl Brown (18)
David Steven Brown (25)
Henry Thomas Burke (47)
Peter Andrew Burkett (24)
Paul William Carlile (19)
Raymond Thomas Chapman (50)
Gary Christopher Church (19)
Joseph Clark (29)
Paul Clark (18)
Gary Collins (22)
Stephen Paul Copoc (20)
Tracey Elizabeth Cox (23
James Philip Delaney (19)
Christopher Barry Devonside (18)
Christopher Edwards (29)
Vincent Michael Fitzsimmons (34)
Thomas Steven Fox (21)
Jon-Paul Gilhooley (10)
Barry Glover (27)
Ian Thomas Glover (20)
Derrick George Godwin (24)
Roy Harry Hamilton (34)
Philip Hammond (14)
Eric Hankin (33)
Gary Harrison (27)
Stephen Francis Harrison (31)
Peter Andrew Harrison (15)
David Hawley (39)
James Robert Hennessy (29)
Paul Anthony Hewitson (26)
Carl Darren Hewitt (17)
Nicholas Michael Hewitt (16)
Sarah Louise Hicks (19)
Victoria Jane Hicks (15)
Gordon Rodney Horn (20)
Arthur Horrocks (41)

Thomas Howard (39)
Thomas Anthony Howard (14)
Eric George Hughes (42)
Alan Johnston (29)
Christine Anne Jones (27)
Gary Philip Jones (18)
Richard Jones (25)
Nicholas Peter Joynes (27)
Anthony Peter Kelly (29)
Michael David Kelly (38)
Carl David Lewis (18)
David William Mather (19)
Brian Christopher Mathews (38)
Francis Joseph McAllister (27)
John McBrien (18)
Marion Hazel McCabe (21)
Joseph Daniel McCarthy (21)
Peter McDonnell (21)
Alan McGlone (28)
Keith McGrath (17)
Paul Brian Murray (14)
Lee Nicol (14)
Stephen Francis O'Neill (17)
Jonathon Owens (18)
William Roy Pemberton (23)
Carl William Rimmer (21)
David George Rimmer (38)
Graham John Roberts (24)
Steven Joseph Robinson (17)
Henry Charles Rogers (17)
Colin Andrew Hugh William Sefton (23)
Inger Shah (38)
Paula Ann Smith (26)
Adam Edward Spearritt (14)
Philip John Steele (15)
David Leonard Thomas (23)
Patrick John Thompson (35)
Peter Reuben Thompson (30)
Stuart Paul William Thompson (17)
Peter Francis Tootle (21)
Christopher James Traynor (26)
Martin Kevin Traynor (16)
Kevin Tyrrell (15)
Colin Wafer (19)
Ian David Whelan (19)
Martin Kenneth Wild (29)
Kevin Daniel Williams (15)
Graham John Wright (17)

ACKNOWLEDGEMENTS

A big 'thumbs up' to Mike Burrows for his time, commitment and innovative art work.

Cheers to all the sacked Liverpool dockers
From the CASA bar, Hope St. (for singing along to Beatles songs while we're trying to write upstairs)

Happy days to the Football arts initiative for the wedge

A 'nice one' to Chris at flexipress for continually getting his arse into gear.

And a 'Top of the world' Kirkby Cagney thank you to Peter (Wacker) Carney for his continued support and for whacking out the deal.
(It takes a scouse activist to make things happen)
It couldn't have happened without you, lad.